4/9/14 Penworthy $21.96

My first book of Farm animals

by Miranda Smith

Natural history consultant:
Dr. Kim Dennis-Bryan, F.Z.S.

An Hachette UK Company
www.hachette.co.uk

First published in Great Britain in 2013 by Ticktock, an imprint of Octopus Publishing Group Ltd,
Endeavour House, 189 Shaftesbury Avenue, London, WC2H 8JY.
www.octopusbooks.co.uk
www.octopusbooksusa.com
www.ticktockbooks.com

Distributed in the USA by Hachette Book Group USA, 237 Park Avenue, New York, NY 10017, USA.

Distributed in Canada by Canadian Manda Group, 165 Dufferin Street, Toronto, Ontario, Canada M6K 3H6.

ISBN 978 1 84898 743 2

Printed and bound in China

1 3 5 7 9 10 8 6 4 2

Cover photography: front, main, Jack Sullivan/Alamy; all others, iStockphoto/Thinkstock;
back, above left, DenisNata/Fotolia; above right, Fuse/Thinkstock; below left, iStockphoto/Thinkstock;
below center, George Doyle/Stockbyte/Thinkstock; below right, iStockphoto/Thinkstock

Contents

Words that appear in **bold** are explained in the glossary.

Meet the farm animals

All around the world, people keep animals on farms. Some farmers keep several different types of animals, while others raise only one type, such as horses.

Chickens and ducks are often seen in farmyards and farm ponds. In the fields and on the prairies, cattle and sheep graze.

Other animals work for the farmer. Alpacas (left) provide wool but also carry heavy loads. And sheepdogs round up sheep and other animals in the fields.

What farm animals eat

To raise healthy animals, farmers make sure that they provide the right food. They either supply special animal feed that contains everything the animals need, or they make sure that the animals can find the right plants to eat out in the open.

Look for these pictures in your book, and they will tell you what kind of food each animal eats.

Plants

Meat (other animals or bugs)

Fish

Where farm animals live

Some animals live in hot places. Others live in cold places. The different types of places where animals live are called habitats. Many animals are specially adapted to be able to survive in the heat or cold of their particular habitat.

Look for these pictures in your book, and they will tell you in what kind of habitat each animal lives.

Deserts: hot, dry, sandy places where it hardly ever rains

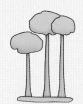
Deciduous forests: forests with trees that lose their leaves in winter

Lakes, ponds, rivers, or streams: freshwater habitats

Rainforests: warm forests with lots of rain

Grasslands: dry places covered with grass

Polar lands: cold, frozen places at the very top and bottom of Earth

Mountains: high, rocky places

Coniferous forests: cold forests with trees that stay green all year

Oceans: a saltwater habitat that covers most of Earth

What farm animals do for us

Farmers raise many animals for us to eat, but their skins, feathers, wool, and even dung are also part of our everyday lives. Look through the book to see what each animal provides for us.

Meat
Most meat is named after the animal it comes from. For example, buffalo meat is buffalo. Some meat is described differently:

cattle = beef, veal, brisket
deer = venison
elk = elk, venison
goat = goat, cabrito, chevon, capretto
llama = llama, charqui (dried meat)
pig = bacon, pork, ham
sheep = lamb, mutton

Eggs
Lots of birds, such as chickens and ducks, lay eggs for us to eat.

Feathers and down
Used inside duvets, pillows, and coats to keep us warm and on arrows to help them fly.

Dairy products
Many animals are raised for their milk, which is also made into cheese and yogurt.

Bristles and hair
Used for hairbrushes and paintbrushes, as well as makeup brushes and cleaning brushes.

Skins
Used for clothing, bags, laces for shoes, as drum skins, or as a floor or wall covering.

Wool and silk
The fur from animals and thread from insects is knitted or woven into clothes that we buy.

Pets
Many farm animals make good pets.

Dung
Animal droppings are used for fertilizer and are sometimes dried and burned as fuel.

Medicine
Some parts of animals, such as antlers, are used to make medicines.

Zoos and safari parks
Farmers provide animals – especially rare breeds – to zoos and safari parks.

Working animals
Lots of animals help farmers by guarding or rounding up other animals, or by catching fish or mice.

To pull heavy loads
Strong animals also help farmers by pulling carts, ploughs, and other heavy loads.

To carry loads
Pack animals, such as camels and llamas, are used to carry heavy loads for people.

Oil
Oil made from animal fat is used to make cosmetics and perfume. It is also used in medicines.

To hunt
Some animals are hunted for sport then eaten as food.

For pearls
Shellfish such as oysters or mussels are used to develop pearls.

To ride
Animals such as horses are kept on farms for people to ride.

To breed
Farmers keep some animals to sell to other people so that they can breed them.

To win prizes
Some farm animals are entered in competitions, such as "Best in Breed."

Chicken

There are probably more chickens in the world than any other kind of bird. They are descended from wild red junglefowl that live in Asia.

Why are chickens farmed?

Eggs

Feathers

Meat

Male chickens are called cockerels or roosters. Many of them have long tails and colored feathers on their necks and backs.

Fantastic fact!

Chickens are the closest living relative of the dinosaur Tyrannosaurus rex.

Chickens live together in flocks. They can fly only short distances.

Female chickens are called hens, and they lay eggs.

Hens specially bred for laying eggs can produce up to 320 eggs a year. Farmers collect the eggs and sell them as food.

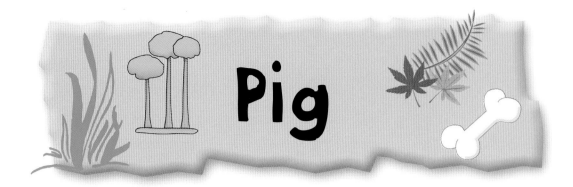

Pig

Why are pigs farmed?

Meat

Skins

Bristles for brushes

Pigs are farmed for their meat, which is called pork, ham, or bacon. Many pigs are kept in pens or sheds. Others, called **free-range** pigs, can wander about.

In warm weather, pigs roll in mud to keep cool. The mud also protects their skin from insect bites and sunburn.

Fantastic fact!

More than 1 billion pigs live on farms around the world.

Pigs are **omnivores**, which means they eat plants, animals, and even insects. They root around for food with their snouts.

Males are called boars, and females are called sows. Pigs come in lots of colors. Some have patterns or spots, and some have curly tails.

Rabbit

Rabbits are farmed all around the world. Some farmers **breed** rabbits to sell as pets, while others raise them for meat and wool. Rabbits are easy to look after and eat grass, vegetables, and hay.

This Angora rabbit will be combed or clipped for its wool, which is warmer, lighter, and fluffier than sheep's wool.

Fantastic fact!

Wild rabbits are a farmland **pest** because they cause damage to crops.

Why are rabbits farmed?

 Wool

 Skins

 Pets

 Meat

Today there are more than 50 breeds of **domestic** rabbit.

The female rabbit, or doe, can give birth three times each year. Rabbits have large litters of up to 10 babies, or kittens.

Goose

Why are geese farmed?

Eggs

Feathers

Meat

Many farm geese are white with an orange bill and orange legs. They make good guards in the farmyard and will honk and attack intruders.

Young geese are called goslings. When they are only one day old, they are able to dive and swim underwater.

The male is called a gander, and the female is called a goose or hen.

Fantastic fact!

Geese can live more than 30 years.

The Embden goose is one of the most popular breeds. It is very tall – up to 3.3 feet (1 meter) – and does not mind the cold.

It mates for life, and the female lays 30 to 40 eggs a year.

Worm

Worms are some of the most useful animals on Earth. As they tunnel, they loosen the soil or sand, helping the air to circulate. Their droppings **fertilize** the soil and help new plants to grow.

Some farmers raise worms on vast farms. Earthworms live in banks of soil, and lugworms like muddy sand on beaches.

Fantastic fact!

Worms eat up to 50 percent of their own body weight every day.

Why are worms farmed?

Composting vegetables and plant matter

Bait for fishing

Bird and wildlife food

Gardeners buy worms from worm farms to add to their **compost** bins. Worms love all kinds of waste matter, including kitchen scraps.

Worms pass kitchen and garden waste through their gut to make compost that gardeners dig into the soil.

Turkey

Turkeys are popular farm birds. They are eaten on special occasions such as Thanksgiving and Christmas.

Most farmers keep turkeys in large barns. They are allowed to wander freely about the barns, which may contain tens of thousands of birds.

Fantastic fact!

An adult turkey has about 3,500 feathers.

Why are turkeys farmed?

Meat

Feathers

Droppings for fertilizer

Male turkeys fan their tail feathers to attract females, and their head and neck become red and blue.

The males are called toms or gobblers. They make a "gobble gobble" sound. The females, or hens, make a clucking sound.

Moose

Moose are the largest members of the deer family. They have big noses and shoulders, and a large flap of skin under their necks, called a "bell." In Russia, farmers keep moose for their milk.

Mother moose, or cows, give birth to their calves in April or May. The farmers take the babies away from the cows and bottle-feed them.

Fantastic fact!

Powdered antler, called antler velvet, is used in Chinese medicine as a health remedy.

Why are moose farmed?

Milk

Antler velvet for medicine

For zoos and safari parks

Male moose are called bulls. Every summer, a bull moose grows a new pair of antlers. The farmers cut off the antlers when they are still soft.

Goat

Why are goats farmed?

Milk, cheese, and yogurt

Wool

Skins

Meat

Dung

Goats have been farmed for their milk, meat, and fur for 10,000 years. Even their **dung** is useful as it makes a good fertilizer for gardens and fuel for fires.

Herds of **dairy** goats are kept in stables during winter and in fields close to the milking shed in summer.

Goats are browsing animals, which means they feed on woody shrubs and leaves.

Fantastic fact!

Goats have horizontal slits for pupils, so they can look around without turning their heads.

The males have beards and are called bucks or billy goats. The females are called does or nanny goats. A baby goat is called a kid.

Dairy Cow

Cows have been bred for their milk for thousands of years. Today most dairy cows are kept in large sheds with outdoor yards. Some are let out into the fields for part of the year to graze on the grass.

Cows are milked twice a day in a milking parlor. Their udders are attached to suction cups from a milking machine.

Fantastic fact!

Milking machines can milk more than 100 cows an hour.

Why are cows farmed?

 Milk, cheese, and yogurt

Meat

 Skins

 Dung

Holstein cows are more than 4.6 feet (1.4 meters) tall. They give birth to one calf and, if milked, will produce milk for three years. In the U.S., Holsteins provide 90 percent of all the milk sold.

Duck

Why are ducks farmed?

Eggs

Meat

Feathers

Pets

Ducks are bred for their eggs, meat, and feathers. Some are raised in sheds, while others roam the farmyard and swim in ponds.

Fantastic fact!

Ducks lay more eggs when there is more daylight.

Around 5 to 12 ducklings hatch out from a **clutch** of eggs. They are able to swim almost immediately.

26

When ducks are kept outside, the farmers clip the feathers on one wing once a year to stop them flying away.

The ducks spread **preen** oil from a gland near their tail to make their feathers waterproof for swimming.

Baboon

In southern Africa farmers have trained baboons to look after their animals. Baboons are strong, intelligent monkeys that spend most of their time on the ground.

Male baboons have fearsome teeth. They yawn to display their teeth, or bark loudly. This scares away other males or animals that threaten them.

Fantastic fact!

While some baboons are farmers' friends, wild baboons often eat crops and sometimes even sheep and goats.

Baboons help farmers by looking after…

Goats   Sheep

Farmers rescue **orphan** baboons, then feed and teach them to protect their herds. This young baboon is looking after baby goats.

Horse

Horses were once the busiest animals on the farm. They pulled carts and ploughs, and carried heavy loads. Today, this work is done by machines.

Cart horses are the largest and strongest of all the horses. They can pull heavy loads many times their own weight. Some farmers still use cart horses to plough their fields.

Fantastic fact!

Horses can sleep both standing up and lying down.

Why do farmers keep horses?

 To carry people and pull ploughs and carts

 To carry heavy loads

 To herd sheep

 Meat

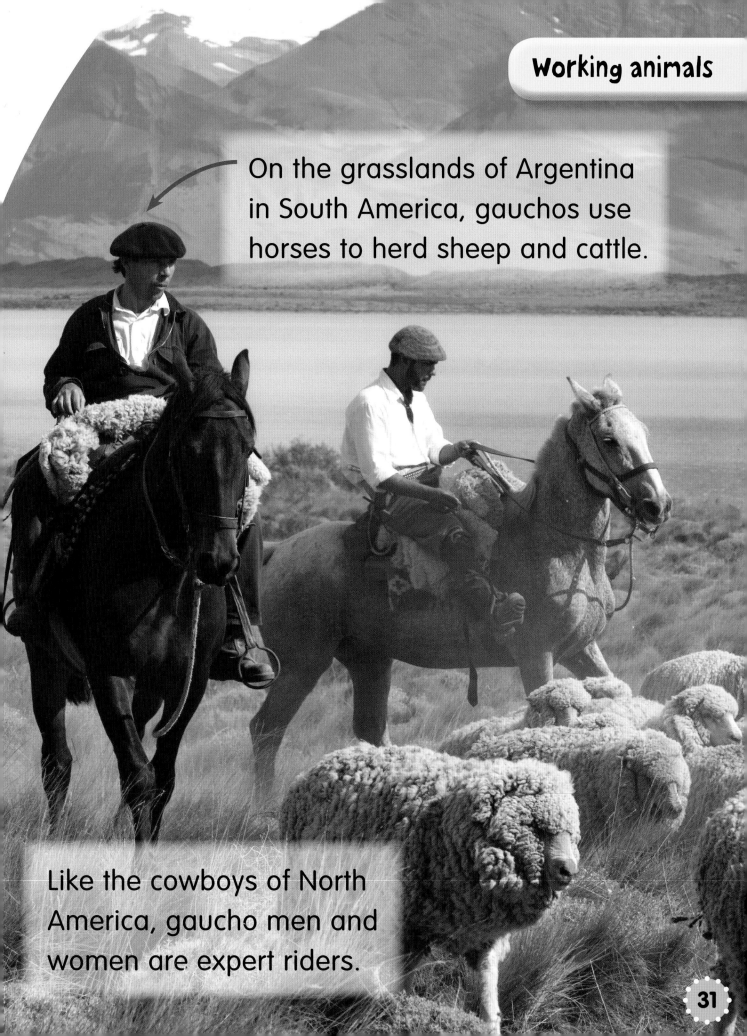

On the grasslands of Argentina in South America, gauchos use horses to herd sheep and cattle.

Like the cowboys of North America, gaucho men and women are expert riders.

Reindeer

Why are reindeer herded?

Milk

Meat

Antler velvet for medicine

Skins

To pull loads

Reindeer, also known as caribou, live in the snowy north, including the Arctic, northern Europe and Asia, and Alaska and Canada.

Reindeer can pull up to twice their own weight. They are used to pull the sleds or sleighs that belong to the herders.

Reindeer have hair covering their nose to keep it from getting frostbite.

Fantastic fact!

Both male and female reindeer have antlers, but the females' antlers are smaller.

Reindeer have been herded
by local peoples for centuries.
They have thick, warm coats
and large hooves that act
like snowshoes.

Llama

Why are llamas farmed?

To carry heavy loads

To guard sheep

Wool

Skins

Dung for fuel

Meat

Llamas are descended from the wild guanaco, a member of the camel family. Llamas have been used as **pack animals** for thousands of years.

Pack trains of llamas move heavy loads over the high passes in the Andes Mountains of South America.

Fantastic fact!

Llamas spit, hiss, or kick if there is something they do not like.

Large herds of llamas are kept for their wool. They have thick fur that is brown, black, or white.

Their fine undercoat is used to make clothes. The coarser outer hair is used to weave rugs, blankets, and rope.

Camel

There are two kinds of camel. The dromedary camel of the Middle East and Africa has one hump on its back and the Bactrian camel of central Asia has two.

Camels have been used to transport people and their goods in desert lands for more than 4,000 years. They have wide feet that help them to walk on sand and rocky surfaces.

Why do farmers keep camels?

To carry goods and people

Milk, cheese, and yogurt

Meat

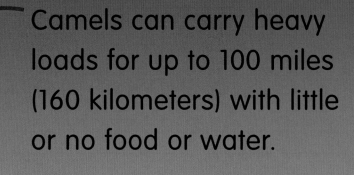

Camels can carry heavy loads for up to 100 miles (160 kilometers) with little or no food or water.

Their humps store fat that they use for food. When they reach water, they can drink up to 13 gallons (15 liters) at a time.

Ox

Farmers use the ox as a kind of living tractor. The animal is extremely strong and can pull a heavier load for longer than a horse.

In some parts of the world, pairs of oxen are used for ploughing. They are tied, or **yoked**, together.

Oxen are good at working in muddy and wet conditions.

Why do farmers keep oxen?

To pull ploughs and carts

Oxen are adult male cattle
that have been taught to work.
They pull carts or machinery and
pull up tree stumps. Sometimes
they are even ridden.

Cormorant

In China and Japan, some people fish using cormorants. These large, sharp-beaked birds dive into the waters of lakes and rivers at night.

Cormorants chase their fish **prey** underwater. They can stay there for more than a minute.

Their feathers are not completely waterproof, so they hold them out to dry when they are out of the water.

Fantastic fact!

Each bird can hold up to six fish in its long throat at a time.

Cormorants help fishermen...

To catch fish

The fisherman ties a string at the bottom of the bird's long neck. This stops the bird from swallowing any large fish that the fisherman wants.

The bird spits out all the fish, but gets one of the catch afterwards, as a reward.

Donkey

Why do farmers keep donkeys?

To carry goods

Milk

Meat

Donkeys are very strong and act as pack animals for farmers all over the world. They can carry heavy loads for long distances.

The Masai people of east Africa keep donkeys alongside their cattle, sheep, and goats. They use the donkeys to carry water and transport goods.

Fantastic fact!

Donkeys are often kept in fields with horses because they help to keep the horses calm.

Donkeys are descended from the African wild ass. They are tough and strong working animals.

Donkeys are related to horses and zebras. They can be stubborn, but work well with people they know.

Donkeys are **herbivores** and can eat tough, almost inedible plants.

Silkworm

The silkworm is the **larva** that hatches out from the eggs of a silk moth. It produces silk that people spin into beautiful, colorful, and shiny material.

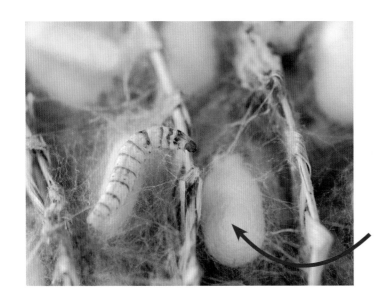

Farmers place the silkworms in straw trays. The silkworms spit the threads of silk out of tiny holes in their jaws to spin the **cocoons**.

The Chinese have been breeding silkworms to harvest silken thread for more than 5,000 years.

Fantastic fact!

The silkworm can spin a cocoon in three days, and a cocoon is made up of 1,200 threads.

Why are silkworms farmed?

Silk

Silkworms feed on the leaves of the mulberry tree.

They eat continuously until they are ready to spin themselves into a cocoon made of raw silk.

Sheepdog

Some sheepdogs, also called **herding** dogs or working dogs, are trained to herd sheep. Others are raised to protect and guard them.

Border collies work alone or in pairs. They move the sheep around at the farmer's commands.

Herding dogs are trained to respond to the farmer's whistles or words.

Fantastic fact!

Dogs are also used to herd cattle, reindeer, and even geese!

Why do farmers keep sheepdogs?

To herd flocks of sheep

To act as guard dogs

Many breeds make good herding dogs. Border collies are bright, energetic, and hardworking. They take five to nine months to train.

Cat

Why do farmers keep cats?

To catch rats and mice

Farm cats, also known as barn cats, protect grain stores and barns from rats and mice. Cats are **carnivores**, or meat-eaters, and they are very clever hunters.

The farm cats prowl around farm buildings and nearby fields looking for something to eat.

Fantastic fact!

Most farm cats are semiwild and do not make good pets.

They catch their prey with their sharp claws, but usually kill it with a single bite.

Cats have very good hearing and excellent eyesight.

They can hear a rustle in the hay or spot the flick of a mouse's tail from a distance.

Sheep

Sheep were one of the first animals to be farmed. They live all over the world, either in fenced fields or wandering free on open **pasture**.

Farmers **shear** their sheep in spring or early summer, cutting off the thick, woolly **fleece**.

Fantastic fact!

A professional shearer can shear a sheep in less than 2 minutes, removing the fleece in one piece.

The wool is cleaned, and the **fibers** are spun into woollen yarn.

Why are sheep farmed?

Wool

Milk, cheese, and yogurt

Meat

Sheepskins

50

The females, or ewes, usually give birth in spring. The ewes feed their lambs on milk until they are old enough to eat grass. A lamb is fully grown after a year.

Ostrich

Ostriches have been farmed for more than 150 years in South Africa. Today they are farmed in many other places, too. In some countries jockeys ride ostriches in races using saddles and reins.

Ostriches lay the largest eggs of all birds, but they are the smallest in relation to the size of the bird. The egg can be up to 8 inches (20 centimeters) long, and the shell is very hard.

Fantastic fact!

An ostrich is the largest living bird, growing up to 7.9 feet (2.4 meters) tall.

Why are ostriches farmed?

 Eggs

 Skins

 Feathers

 Oil for cosmetics

 Meat

Ostriches eat insects, seeds, and other plant matter. They do not have teeth, so they swallow pebbles to help grind up food in their **gizzard**.

Pheasant and partridge

Why are game birds farmed?

Meat

Feathers

Sport

Pheasants and partridges are **game birds**. In some countries they are bred on special estates to be shot for sport and food.

Partridges live together in coveys, or groups, of between 6 and 15 birds. Their wings make a whirring sound when they fly.

Partridges live on the ground and **forage** for leaves to build their nests and seeds and insects to eat.

Fantastic fact!

Fishermen use pheasant and partridge feathers to make **flies** to catch fish.

The male common pheasant is a colorful bird with a long tail.

On many farms, the chicks, which are called poults, are kept in outside pens, or **aviaries**.

When the birds are grown, the farmers sell them or release them into the fields for hunters.

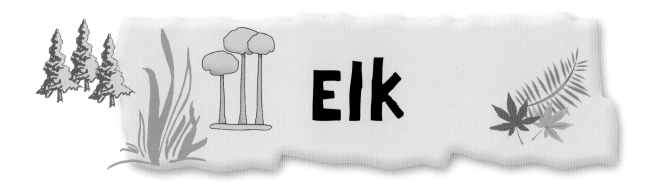

Elk

The North American elk, or wapiti, are farmed for their meat. Some **ranches** raise the animals so that people can hunt them and take their antlers as trophies.

Elk males are called bulls. Their "bugling," or calling, establishes their **territory** and can be heard over long distances.

One bull will mate with 20 to 40 cows, which will each give birth to a single calf.

Fantastic fact!

Elk antlers may be 4 feet (1.2 meters) tall and weigh over 40 pounds (18 kilograms).

Why are elk farmed?

 Meat

 Skins

 Antler velvet for medicine

 To hunt

Elk eat whatever they can find over their **range**, including shrubs, leaves, and bark.

They eat a lot of rich grass in summer, which allows them to store fat for winter.

Deer

Why are deer farmed?

Meat

Skins

Antlers

Musk perfume

Antler velvet for medicine

Wild deer have always been hunted for their meat and skins. The deer are kept in fields or paddocks, or roam the hills.

Deer can be dangerous, so farmers need to understand their behavior. Red deer stags fight over females in the **rutting**, or mating, season.

They sometimes use their large antlers to attack people, too.

Fantastic fact!

New Zealand has the largest number of deer farms in the world.

Deer eat grasses, twigs, and leaves, but they like legumes and flowering plants best.

Farmers make sure there is plenty of the correct type of plants in the hills or fields.

59

Beef cattle

Beef cattle are farmed all over the world for their meat. They graze in large herds on grass in fields. The herds are moved regularly to find fresh pasture.

Brazil exports more beef than any other country in the world. Vaqueiros, or cowherds, move the herds of cattle to find new pastures.

Fantastic fact!

About 90 percent of all cattle in Australia are used for beef.

Why are cattle farmed?

Meat

Skins

These cattle are **grazing** in the **outback** in Queensland, Australia.

Farmers select special breeds that can live in the hot, dry conditions on the cattle stations.

Bison

Why are bison farmed?

Meat

Skins

Horns

Centuries ago, tens of millions of wild bison wandered across the plains of North America. Native Americans hunted them for their meat and hides.

Later, settlers hunted the bison almost to **extinction** until there were less than 1,000 left.

Fantastic fact!

Bison are wild animals that cannot be tamed, so many farmers find them difficult to handle.

Today, the numbers are up to 500,000 because ranchers and **conservationists** decided to breed them.

Bison are very big. The bulls weigh around 2,000 pounds (900 kilograms) – as much as a small car. Their thick fur protects them in the coldest winters.

They run very fast – they are even able to outrun a horse, so are sometimes difficult to round up.

Salmon and trout

Salmon and trout are farmed in fish **hatcheries**. Some farmers use fish cages that they place in open water. Others use specially built ponds or tanks to raise the fish.

Young salmon, or fry, are hatched from eggs and raised in freshwater tanks. At one year of age they are moved to floating sea cages on the coast.

The salmon are fed in the cages for a year, and then taken to market.

Fantastic fact!

More than half of the world's salmon comes from fish farms.

Why are salmon and trout farmed?

Meat

Fish oil

Fertilizer

When trout fry hatch, they are first kept in tanks and then moved to a pond or pool.

Freshwater trout are raised from fingerlings, or baby fish, until they are about 14 inches (35 centimeters) long.

Crocodile

It is not easy being a farmer, especially a farmer of crocodiles. They grow up to 16 feet (5 meters) in length, weigh nearly 2,000 pounds, and have 66 sharp teeth.

Crocodiles are carnivores. They move slowly on land, but are very dangerous in the water.

They need water to cool their bodies, but will also open their mouths to get rid of excess heat.

Fantastic fact!

A female crocodile can lay a clutch of up to 60 eggs at a time.

66

Crocodiles were once farmed for their skin, but today they are eaten, too. Saltwater crocodiles are the largest in the world and are farmed in Africa, parts of Asia, and Australia.

Mussels and oysters

Mussels and oysters are **bivalves**, meaning their shell has two parts, called valves, that hinge together. They are farmed as food and to grow pearls.

Oysters are grown from larvae. When they reach 1.2 inches (30 millimeters), the young oysters are glued to mats and then put on the seabed to grow for nine months.

Fantastic fact!

The Chinese were the first to raise oysters in artificial ponds.

Why are mussels and oysters farmed?

 To eat

 Pearls

Mussels live in large clusters, attaching themselves to rocks or other hard surfaces with small threads.

Farmers attach them to ropes hung from large floats or long poles in the sea. They are harvested after three years.

Water buffalo

Why are water buffalo farmed?

To pull heavy loads

Milk, cheese, and yogurt

Meat

Oil for cooking

Dung for fuel

There are two types of water buffalo, the swamp buffalo and river buffalo. They have large horns and are powerful animals, used by farmers to pull heavy loads.

Swamp buffalo have wide, curving horns.

This swamp buffalo is being used to pull the plough in a rice **paddy**. Its large, splayed feet help it to move steadily through the muddy water.

Fantastic fact!

River buffalo milk has twice the fat content of cow's milk. It is used to make cheese called mozzarella.

River buffalo have been bred for their milk. They have curled horns.

DZO

Why are dzos farmed?

To pull heavy loads

Milk

Skins

Meat

A dzo is a cross between a yak and a domestic cow. The animals were first bred in Tibet for their strength. They obey orders easily, so they are perfect farm animals.

With their shaggy coats, dzos are able to withstand the harsh weather of high, mountainous countries such as Tibet and Mongolia.

Fantastic fact!

Dzos are larger and stronger than their yak and cow parents.

The males are called dzos and are usually used by farmers to pull ploughs or as pack animals.

The females are called dzomos. They provide the farmer with meat, as well as milk that is made into butter and cheese.

Kuvasz

Shepherds use this dog to look after their sheep, cattle, horses, and even emus. It was bred in Hungary as a guard dog.

A kuvasz is fiercely protective and will chase wolves, bears, bobcats, coyotes, and cougars if they threaten the flock or herd.

The word *kuvasz* means "protector" in Turkish.

Fantastic fact!

Once the dog has bonded with the animals it is herding, it will follow them everywhere.

Why do farmers keep kuvasz dogs?

To guard flocks

As a pet

Shepherds bred the kuvasz to have a light-colored coat so they could see the difference between the dog and a wolf from a distance.

Merino Sheep

Why are merino sheep farmed?

Wool

Milk, cheese, and yogurt

Meat

Merino sheep produce some of the world's softest wools. They were first bred in Spain, but are now farmed in the U.S., South Africa, and Australia.

In Australia, ranches raise enormous flocks of merinos. This is because they survive well in conditions that are too hot and dry for other sheep.

Fantastic fact!

Merino sheep are shorn once a year and produce up to 40 pounds (18 kilograms) of wool.

Males, or rams, have large, curly horns, while the females, or ewes, do not have horns.

All have wrinkly skin and crinkly fleeces, especially around their neck and shoulders. Their fleeces grow up to 4 inches (10 centimeters) in length every year.

Angora goat

The Angora goat is an ancient breed. It is named after Ankara, originally called Angora, in Turkey. Its hair hangs in ringlets from its body. Its soft fleece, called **mohair**, is turned into a soft yarn.

Angora goats are shorn once or twice a year. Mohair is warmer than other yarns.

Fibers from the younger goats are the softest and are used to make clothing.

Fantastic fact!

A single goat produces up to 11 pounds (5 kilograms) of hair a year.

Why are Angora goats farmed?

Mohair

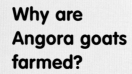
Meat

Farmers keep herds of Angoras in fields where they eat woody weeds.

The goats help the farmer by clearing prickly plants.

Arab horse

Why are Arabs farmed?

To breed

To ride

The Arab, or Arabian, is the oldest breed of horse. The **nomadic** Bedouins of the Arabian peninsula used it to transport themselves and their goods across the desert.

Fantastic fact!

Almost every breed of horse today has some trace of Arab blood.

The light build and stamina of an Arabian makes it the perfect choice of horse for racing.

Today, **stud farms** supply purebred Arab horses to people all over the world for riding and horse racing. They are tough and spirited, with a small, slim head, arched neck, and high tail.

Rhode Island Red

This colorful breed of chicken is raised for meat and eggs, and as show birds to win competitions. It was first bred by **poultry** farmers in Rhode Island more than 100 years ago.

These chickens like to stay together in small groups. They forage in the grass for insects, worms, and seeds.

Fantastic fact!

A single Rhode Island Red hen can lay more than 300 dark brown eggs a year.

Why are Rhode Island Reds farmed?

 Eggs

 Feathers

 To win prizes

 Meat

Rhode Island Red feathers are a dark, rich, glossy red, often with white streaks. The males, or roosters, have wonderful red **combs**.

They are large, independent, and fierce birds and will attack human or animal strangers.

Jacob sheep

Why are Jacob sheep farmed?

Wool

Meat

Skins

As pets

This very ancient, rare breed of sheep has a white coat with dark brown spots. It is multihorned and can look like a goat.

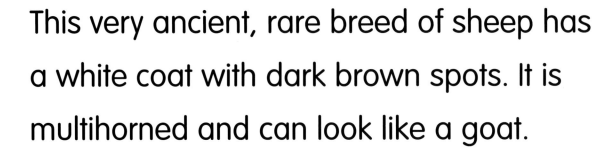

Most Jacobs have four horns, although some have two and others have six. The males, or rams, have much larger horns than the females, or ewes.

Their soft, colorful fleeces are very popular with hand-knitters and weavers.

Fantastic fact!

Each Jacob has individual markings, which allows a shepherd to recognize it from a distance.

All Jacob sheep have brown and white fleeces, but with varying amounts of each color.

Most sheep breeds give birth to one or two lambs, but Jacobs often have triplets or quadruplets.

Aberdeen Angus

Aberdeen Angus are a highly valued breed of cattle famous for their meat. They were developed in Scotland and were originally known as "Angus doddies."

The Angus cows produce lots of milk for their calves – usually one calf a year. Sometimes they have twins.

Fantastic fact!

In Australia, 30 percent of all cattle sold are Angus.

There are two colors of Angus: black and, less common, red. Neither has any horns.

Why are Aberdeen Angus bulls farmed?

Meat

The good-natured
Aberdeen Angus
bulls grow fast.

They can grow to
2,790 pounds (1,270
kilograms) in weight.

Bali duck

Why are Bali ducks farmed?

Pest control

Eggs

Meat

Dung

As pets

The Bali duck is raised by duck farmers on the island of Bali in Indonesia to work in the fields and for its eggs, which are sold in the local markets.

Bali ducks waddle in orderly lines to work in the rice paddies. Balinese people admire them and think they are intelligent creatures.

The ducks help to keep the crops disease-free as they eat insect pests. They also fertilize the rice paddies with their dung.

Fantastic fact!

Bali duck meat is expensive and is eaten only on special occasions on the island.

88

Every day, the farmers drive their Bali ducks to the stepped rice terraces on their farms.

The ducks search the muddy waters for leftover rice straw and grains, worms, and small water animals.

Alpaca

Why are alpacas farmed?

Wool

Meat

As pets

Alpacas are kept in herds that graze on the high plains of the Andes Mountains in South America. They are closely related to the llama, but they are smaller.

Alpacas are social animals and herds can be very large. They eat grass and hay throughout the year. They also need shelter to allow them to get out of the rain.

Fantastic fact!

An alpaca fleece can weigh up to 11 pounds (5 kilograms).

Alpacas are bred
for their wool,
which is made
into blankets and
clothing, including
ponchos.

They are all
different colors,
from white to
browns, grays,
and blacks.

Highland cattle

Herds of Highland cattle, called folds, are seen on mountain slopes all over the world. They thrive and breed outside in places with high rainfall and strong winds.

The males, or bulls, keep a close watch over their folds, guiding them through swollen rivers or over marshy ground.

The cows protect calves against **predators**, hiding them in tall grass and returning to feed them twice a day.

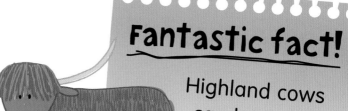

Fantastic fact!

Highland cows can have up to 15 calves in their lifetime.

Why are Highland cattle farmed?

 Meat

Milk and other dairy products

 Skins

Highlanders have thick, double-hair coats. The soft undercoat can grow up to 13 inches (33 centimeters) long and keeps them warm.

The outer coat keeps them waterproof. A long fringe of hair shields their eyes against snow and driving rain.

Glossary

aviary (plural: aviaries) A netted open space where birds are kept.

bivalve Shellfish that have two shells, joined by a hinge.

breed A particular type of animal – for example, a Holstein cow or a Jacob sheep; to produce young.

carnivore An animal that eats meat.

clutch The number of eggs that are produced at one time.

cocoon The silky envelope spun by the larvae of insects such as silk moths to protect themselves while they are developing into adults.

comb The flap of skin that grows on the top of the heads of cockerels.

compost A mixture of decaying things, such as leaves or dung, that is used for fertilizing soil.

conservationist A person who works to protect animals and their environment.

dairy A place where milk is kept or where butter and cheese are made. Dairy cows are kept for their milk.

domestic Describes an animal that is kept by people.

dung Animal droppings. Also known as manure. It contains material that is good for the soil.

extinction The dying out of a particular kind, or species, of animal.

fertilize Add nutrients and minerals to the soil to make plants grow well.

fibers Long, fine continuous threads.

fleece The coat of a sheep or goat.

flies Hooks that are made to look like flies and used by fishermen to catch fish.

forage To move around searching for food.

free-range Describes animals that are allowed to roam freely looking for food.

game bird A bird hunted mainly for sport.

gizzard Part of a bird's stomach that helps to grind up food with swallowed stones or grit.

grazing Feeding on grass in fields.

hatchery (plural: hatcheries) A special place where eggs are kept warm and hatched.

herbivore An animal that is a plant-eater.

herding Rounding up and moving a group of animals such as cattle, sheep, or reindeer.

irrigation The watering of growing crops by a farmer.

larva The second stage in the life of an insect, the stage between the egg and an adult.

mohair The coat of an Angora goat.

nomadic Describes herdsmen who travel from place to place in search of food or to find grass for animals.

omnivore An animal that eats plants and meat.

orphan An animal that has lost its parents, possibly because they were killed.

outback The remote bush country of Australia.

pack animal An animal bred and used to carry heavy loads.

paddy An irrigated or flooded field where rice is grown.

pasture An area covered with grass or other plants on which animals can graze.

pest An insect or other small creature that harms or destroys plants.

poultry Birds such as chickens or ducks that are kept for eggs and meat.

predator An animal that hunts and eats other animals.

preen To clean, oil, and smooth feathers. Birds keep their feathers in a healthy state by preening.

prey An animal that is hunted and eaten by another animal.

ranch (plural: ranches) A large farm, especially in North America and Australia, where animals such as sheep, ostriches, and horses are bred and raised.

range The area of land over which an animal roams.

rutting The behavior of animals such as deer when they are mating.

shear To remove the fleece of a sheep by cutting and clipping. Other animals such as goats are shorn.

stud farm A farm where horses are bred.

territory An area of land where an animal or group of animals lives, and which they guard.

yoked Joined together by a wooden frame called a yoke. Oxen and water buffalo are often yoked when they pull a plough.

Index

Picture credits

Alamy/A & J Visage 40; Bon Appetit 68; Christoph Bosch 63; Bruce Coleman Inc./Jean-Claude Carton 13; David R. Frazier Photolibrary, Inc. 31; Tim Davies 28; Brian Elliott 78; Gaertner 24; Guy Harrop 46; Hemis 69; Wayne Hutchinson 47, 87; Imagebroker 72; JTB Media Creation, Inc. 41; Juniors Bildarchiv GmbH 51, 75; Mike Lane 60; OJO Images Ltd./David Henderson 92; Papilio/Robert Pickett 59; Photoshot Holdings Ltd. 55; David Ridley 84; Pep Roig 71; Dave Stamboulis 73; UK City Images 85; Lisa Young 36; ZUMA Wire Service 16, 17.
Corbis/Yann Arthus-Bertrand 12; Reuters/Katarina Stoltz 20.
FLPA/Bjorn Ullhagen 86.
Fotolia/f3bri 89; Mari_art 81; Elena Moiseeva 43; Mikhail Pogosov 80; Carola Schubbel 74; winni 88.
Getty Images/Paul Harris 32, 33.
NHPA/Martin Harvey 29; Christophe Ratier 42.
Thinkstock/AbelStock.com 56; Design Pics 14; Hemera 9, 18, 27, 50, 67; Hemera Technologies 38; Ingram Publishing 34, 45; iStockphoto 2, 3, 4, 8, 10, 11, 15, 19, 21, 22, 23, 25, 26, 30, 35, 37, 39, 44, 48, 49, 52, 53, 54, 57, 58, 61, 62, 64, 65, 66, 70, 76, 77, 79, 82, 83, 90, 91, 93.

Illustrations
Kait Eaton